The Divine Dispensing for the Divine Economy

Witness Lee

Living Stream Ministry
Anaheim, California

First Edition, December 1990.

ISBN 978-0-87083-558-2

Published by

Living Stream Ministry
2431 W. La Palma Ave., Anaheim, CA 92801 U.S.A.
P. O. Box 2121, Anaheim, CA 92814 U.S.A.

Printed in the United States of America

09   10   11   12   13   14   /   10   9   8   7   6   5   4   3

CONTENTS

PREFACE

This book is composed of messages given by Brother Witness Lee in September 1990 in San Diego and San Bernardino, California. Chapters one through three were given in San Diego on September 15-16, and chapter four was given in San Bernardino on September 23.

CHAPTER ONE

THE DIVINE ECONOMY
AND ITS ACCOMPLISHMENT

Scripture Reading: Eph. 1:9-10; 3:9-11; 1 Tim. 1:3-4; Eph.
1:23; 3:19b; 1:4-5, 7, 11, 13b; 4:30; 1:19-23

THE ECONOMY AND DISPENSING OF GOD

God's economy is His household administration to dispense Himself in Christ into His chosen people that He may
have a house, a household, to express Himself, which household is the church, the Body of Christ (1 Tim. 3:15). The word
for economy, *oikonomia*, is used in the book of Ephesians
three times. In 1:10 and 3:9 it is translated as "dispensation,"
whereas in 3:2 it is translated as "stewardship." God's dispensation is His arrangement, which is His plan or purpose,
His household administration. Ephesians 3:2 speaks of the
stewardship which was given to Paul. As God's servant,
Paul was a steward of God, and God gave him a ministry, a
service, which is called the stewardship. On God's side
oikonomia refers to God's arrangement, God's plan, but on
Paul's side *oikonomia* refers to Paul's stewardship, Paul's
ministry, Paul's service. God's plan, God's arrangement,
eventually becomes Paul's ministry, Paul's stewardship. In
1 Timothy 1:3-4, Paul tells Timothy to charge certain ones
not to teach differently but to teach the dispensation, the
economy, of God. Here it means to teach the arrangement, the
plan, of God.

Dispensation and dispensing refer to two different things.
Dispensing means giving, distributing, or imparting. God has
an economy, and His dispensing is for His economy. God
fulfills His divine economy by His divine dispensing. The
economy of God is the plan and arrangement out of God's

desire and purpose. The dispensing of God is the dispensing and distributing according to God's plan and arrangement.

The Divine Economy in Creation

One of the items of God's economy was His creation of the heavens and the earth. In His creation three categories of life were produced: plant life, animal life, and human life. These three lives beautify the earth. The trees of the garden were not only good for food but also pleasant to the sight (Gen. 2:9). Animal life adds to the beauty of the earth. But without human life, the earth would lack meaning. Human life adds meaning to the entire earth. If man is without God, however, the universe becomes meaningless, because God is the meaning of human life. Without God's life, the universe is meaningless, without a goal, and without a purpose. God has an eternal purpose. While it is certainly true that the unbelievers do not know what God's purpose is, it is also true that many who have been Christians for many years do not know what God's eternal purpose is. They do not know why God created the heavens, the earth, or man. Furthermore, they do not know why God saved them. In order to know the purpose of God, we must get into the depths of the Bible.

The Deepest Layer of the Divine Revelation

The Bible is the divine revelation. Hence, it is not a simple book. It is a profound book. After I got saved, as a young Christian I began to love the Bible. The more I read it, the more I realized that I could not fully understand it. After many years of studying it, I have discovered that the Bible has at least three layers. The first layer is that God loves us. Because He loves us, God gives us blessing, happiness, peace, and especially His salvation. In response to His love, we love God and His Word. This causes us to touch the second layer. The second layer is morality, proper behavior, good character, and spirituality. Most Christians stop here, but this is not the intrinsic or deepest part of the Bible. There is still another layer. God's dispensation is the deepest layer within the Bible.

We may read a verse such as Ephesians 1:10, but have very little understanding of the word *dispensation* in this verse. Verses such as John 3:16 are easily understood by many Christians, but only in a superficial and shallow way. Many appreciate the first part of John 3:16 which says that "God so loved the world that He gave His only begotten Son." But when asked what eternal life is in the latter part of this verse, few have a very accurate understanding. Some would say that eternal life is going to heaven, living in a heavenly mansion, and walking on a golden street within pearly gates to enjoy peace and blessings for eternity. This is mostly a wrong concept of what eternal life is. The salvation of God preached in Christianity is true but very shallow. God's salvation also has layers. These layers include the forgiveness of sins, washing from sin, being redeemed by the blood, being justified through Jesus Christ, and being regenerated. But the deepest layer of God's salvation is God's plan to work Himself into His created, chosen, redeemed, and regenerated people. God's eternal plan is to work Himself into His chosen people so that He becomes their very constituent.

Eating, Digesting, and Assimilating Jesus as Our Spiritual Food

God not only desires that man be His vessel to contain Him (Rom. 9:21, 23; 2 Cor. 4:7), but also wants man to eat, digest, and assimilate Him (John 6:57). When we eat, digest, and assimilate physical food, we are energized and strengthened. The food that we eat is dispensed into our blood, and through the blood into every part of our body. Eventually, the food that we have eaten becomes the fiber, tissue, and cells of our being. In the same way, God's eternal plan is to dispense Himself into us so that He becomes every fiber of our inward being. He wants to be digested and assimilated by us so that He can become the constituent of our inward being.

God created man in His image so that man could contain Him. A container is always in the image or shape of the content it is destined to contain. If the content is round, the container must also be round. The creation of man in God's image is for the dispensing of God into man. After man was created, God placed him in front of the tree of life (Gen. 2:8-9). Then immediately, God warned man about his eating (vv. 16-17). If man ate of the tree of life, he would live; but if he ate of the tree of the knowledge of good and evil, he would die. The tree of life signifies God Himself. Today, God is our food; He is edible. In John 6 Jesus said that He was the bread of life (vv. 35, 48), and in verse 57 He said, "As the living Father sent Me, and I live because of the Father, so he who eats Me shall also live because of Me." We need to eat Jesus.

To be a Christian is more than just repenting of our sins, receiving the forgiveness of sins, being washed by the blood, being justified, and being regenerated. The Christian life also includes growth and maturity. In order to go on from regeneration to maturity, we must eat. Regeneration is the beginning of our spiritual life, but we need to eat after our regeneration. No one can grow without eating. We must eat, digest, and assimilate food daily. Assimilation is the final step of food being dispensed into our being. We need to eat, digest, and assimilate Jesus as our spiritual food day by day.

According to God's economy, God is not only our Savior objectively but also our food subjectively. This is shown by the type of the Passover in Exodus 12. The blood of the Passover lamb was sprinkled on the side posts and the upper doorpost of the houses of the Israelites (v. 7). This signifies the redemption of Christ in its objective aspect. God also charged the children of Israel to eat the meat of the lamb which they had killed (v. 8). Under the covering of the blood of the Passover lamb, they were to eat the flesh of the Passover lamb, not leaving anything for the next day (v. 10). This was one of God's ordinances concerning their eating. In nearly every culture, there are so-called "table manners" which govern the way of eating. According to Exodus 12, one of God's "table manners" was to finish the entire lamb. God would be insulted if there was anything left over until the morning. If there was more lamb than one household could eat, the Israelites were to share the lamb with their neighbor next door (vv. 3-4). This signifies the preaching of the gospel. We should lead our neighboring families to share in God's rich and boundless salvation, which our family cannot exhaust. After the Israelites were filled with the lamb through eating, they were strengthened in order to make their exodus out of Egypt. The Israelites marched out of Egypt, and while they were marching, they were digesting and assimilating the lamb. This digestion and assimilation was the dispensing of the lamb into their being. Through their digestion and assimilation of the Passover lamb, the dispensing of the Passover lamb took place. This dispensed lamb became their strength.

THE DIVINE ECONOMY

The Arrangement of the Eternal Plan of God's Household Administration

The Mystery of God's Will, a Mystery Which from the Ages Has Been Hidden in God, Who Created All Things

The divine economy is the arrangement of the eternal plan of God's household administration (Eph. 1:9-10; 3:9-11; 1 Tim. 1:3-4). The divine economy is the mystery of God's will, a mystery which from the ages has been hidden in God, who created all things (Eph. 1:9; 3:9). It was a mystery because it was not unveiled to any human being in past ages. Adam and Abraham were never told about God's economy. It was hidden in God; therefore, it was a hidden mystery. Men could see the creation, but they could not understand the purpose of the creation. Today this mystery has been unveiled to us.

According to God's Eternal Purpose Made in Christ to Head Up All Things in Christ

The divine economy is according to God's eternal purpose (Eph. 3:11) which He made in Christ to head up all things in Christ (1:10). Today we still cannot see all things headed up in Christ, but we do see this heading up on a small scale. God is heading up the believers of Christ. God's intention is to head up all Christians in Christ to be one. Satan's intention, however, is to divide. Any division, regardless of the reason, must be condemned because division is against God's heading up of all things in Christ.

To Have a Church to Be the Body of Christ as His Fullness for a Corporate Expression of the Processed Triune God

God desires to have a church to be the Body of Christ as His fullness for a corporate expression of the processed Triune God (Eph. 1:23; 3:19b). This is not just a congregation composed of a number of believers. The Body of Christ is an organic Body of a great person—Christ. In order for Christ to have such a Body, He must dispense Himself into His chosen and redeemed people.

THE ACCOMPLISHMENT OF THE DIVINE ECONOMY

The Divine Dispensing of the Divine Trinity

The accomplishment of the divine economy is by the divine dispensing of the Divine Trinity. God is divine, and He is also triune. He is triune in order to complete the steps for the dispensing of Himself into us. To dispense Himself into us, He has taken three steps: the Father's choosing and predestinating, the Son's redeeming, and the Spirit's sealing. These three steps are for God's divine dispensing.

Through the Father's Choosing and Predestinating

The first step of the divine dispensing of the Divine Trinity was the Father's choosing and predestinating (Eph. 1:4-5). The Father chose us in Christ before the foundation of the world that we should be holy. How can we common human beings be holy? We cannot be made holy by our outward actions. Neither can we be holy by being washed. To be washed makes us clean, but to be clean is not to be holy. The only way we can be holy is by a holy element being dispensed into our being. Medical doctors know that our physical bodies need many minerals. If our blood is short of iron, the only way iron can get into our blood is by the food that we eat or drink. In the same way, we become holy by receiving the holy God with His holy nature into our being. His holy element then becomes our element. The Father chose us in Christ before the foundation of the world that we, the chosen ones, may have the Father's holy nature and thus may be sanctified through the dispensing of the Father's holy nature into us, His chosen ones.

The Father's predestinating through Christ is so that the predestinated ones may have His life for their sonship through the dispensing of the Father's divine life into us (Eph. 1:5). To have the sonship implies that we must have God's life. The divine life generates us to be God's sons. As God's sons we have God's life, so we have God's sonship. God the Father imparts Himself into our being as our holy nature to make us holy and as our divine life to make us His sons so that we may have sonship. To be made holy and to receive the sonship are a matter of receiving the divine dispensing. The divine way for us to be made holy and to receive the sonship is by God dispensing Himself into us.

Through the Son's Redeeming

The accomplishment of the divine economy by the divine dispensing of the Divine Trinity is not only through the Father's choosing and predestinating but also through the Son's redeeming (Eph. 1:7). The Son's redeeming is not just outward and objective. It is not just a matter of Christ shedding His blood in order to redeem us and to cleanse us from our sins. The Son's redeeming is much deeper than this. Through the Son's redeeming, the redeemed are put into Christ. We were put in Christ so that we could be made an inheritance of God with Christ as the element and realm of the divine inheritance (Eph. 1:11). We were put in Christ and made an inheritance of God through the dispensing of Christ. It is as if God said, "I have redeemed you and put you into Christ. This Christ will become your element for you to be My inheritance. I do not have any intention to inherit you in your natural being. You are just a sinner. Even though you are redeemed, you are just cleansed. I want to inherit My Son in you. Now you have My Son in you as the element to constitute you into something precious. This will be counted as My inheritance." In order for God to gain such an inheritance, He had to dispense Himself in Christ into our being.

Through the Spirit's Sealing

Ephesians 1 reveals the Father's choosing and predestinating, the Son's redeeming, and the Spirit's sealing (v. 13b). The sealing of the Spirit can be likened to a seal with ink being pressed upon a sheet of paper. The more the ink is applied, the more the paper is saturated and permeated with the ink. Eventually, the entire paper will be sealed, saturated, and permeated with the substance of the ink in the image of the seal. In the same way, the Spirit is saturating and permeating us. The last stanza of hymn #501 in *Hymns* says:

> Thy Spirit will me saturate,
> Every part will God permeate....

This sealing, permeating, and saturating is going on constantly in the believers. As you are reading this chapter, the Spirit is permeating you. The Spirit as the sealing ink remains wet forever. It never dries. The Spirit's sealing saturates the sealed ones through the dispensing of the sealing ink unto, or for, the day of the redemption of their body (Eph. 4:30). The redemption of our body is the transfiguration of our body (Phil. 3:21). Until the transfiguration of our body, the sealing of the Spirit will go on continually to saturate and permeate our entire being.

Issuing in the Church

The issue of the divine dispensing of the Divine Trinity through the Father's choosing and predestinating, the Son's redeeming, and the Spirit's sealing is the church (Eph. 1:22b).

Through the Transmission, the Dispensing,
of the Resurrected and Ascended Christ

The church as the issue of the divine dispensing is through the transmission, the dispensing, of the resurrected and ascended Christ (Eph. 1:19-22a). God's power was wrought in Christ in raising Him from among the dead and seating Him at His right hand in the heavenlies. Christ was raised from among the dead in Hades to the throne of God in the third heaven. Everything was subjected under His feet, and He was made Head over all things to the church. The word *to* in verse 22 implies a transmission. Whatever God has wrought in Christ is transmitted and is being transmitted to the church.

That the Church May Be
the Body of Christ for the Corporate
Expression of the Processed Triune God

This transmission is so that the church may be the Body of Christ, the fullness of the One who fills all in all, for the corporate expression of the processed Triune God (Eph. 1:23).

CHAPTER TWO

THE APOSTLE'S STEWARDSHIP
DISPENSING THE RICHES OF CHRIST
AND CHRIST MAKING HIS HOME
IN THE HEARTS OF THE SAINTS

Scripture Reading: Eph. 3:2-5, 7-11, 14-19

THE FATHER'S CHOOSING, THE SON'S REDEEMING,
AND THE SPIRIT'S SEALING ISSUING IN THE CHURCH

According to chapter one of Ephesians, the church has been constituted for its existence through the dispensing of the Divine Trinity. The dispensing of the Divine Trinity is of the Father as the source (vv. 3-6), of the Son as the course (vv. 7-12), and of the Spirit as the flow (vv. 13-14). The dispensing of the Father as the source includes the Father's choosing (v. 4) and predestination (v. 5). The Father's intention in choosing us is to dispense His holy nature into us so that we may be holy. The Father's predestination is so that we will receive the Father's divine life. Upon receiving the Father's divine life, we are born of God to be His sons in order to enjoy the sonship.

The church is also constituted through the Son's redeeming. The Father chose and predestinated us. Then the Son came in to redeem us. The Son's redeeming brought us into a condition in which we could become the Father's inheritance. God the Father inherits only that which has the divine nature. His inheritance must come up to the standard of His divinity. For this reason, the redemption of Christ must bring us into God Himself. His redemption is not just a matter of redeeming us from sin; it is even more a matter of redeeming us into God Himself, into His very divine element. This divine element constitutes us into a precious treasure for God's inheritance.

The divine dispensing of the Divine Trinity according to Ephesians 1 consummates in the Spirit's sealing (vv. 13-14). The entire being of the complete God reaches our being through the sealing of the Spirit. The sealing of the Spirit saturates the sealed ones. The Spirit as the living seal is also the sealing ink applied to our inward being in the image of the seal. The ink stamped onto a piece of paper will eventually become dry, but the Spirit as the sealing ink remains "wet" all the time unto eternity. Because the Spirit as the sealing ink remains "wet," the Spirit continually saturates and permeates us until our entire being—spirit, soul, and body—is sealed. Eventually, through the divine sealing, we human beings become the expression not only of the God who creates, but also of the regenerating, sanctifying, transforming, and glorifying God. We become His expression, His fullness. This is the aim and goal of the divine economy, God's eternal arrangement as His eternal plan. God desires to make His chosen ones His expression, His fullness, in a corporate way.

FULFILLING OUR STEWARDSHIP
TO DISPENSE THE RICHES OF CHRIST
INTO PEOPLE BY PREACHING THE GOSPEL

The stewardship of the apostle is to dispense, to minister, the unsearchable riches of Christ as the gospel to the nations (Eph. 3:2, 8). Some may think that only the apostle Paul has received this stewardship because he was the top apostle. Many believers also maintain that there have only been twelve apostles throughout church history. This concept is based upon the erroneous teaching of some of the Brethren teachers which stated that the twelve disciples selected by the Lord Jesus were the only apostles. According to this teaching, Paul replaced Judas as the twelfth apostle, instead of Matthias. They say that Matthias was excluded because he was selected by lots and not by Christ directly as Paul was. This teaching, however, is not according to the entire revelation of the New Testament. Acts 1:26 says that after the lot fell upon Matthias, "he was numbered with the eleven apostles." In the next chapter, the Holy Spirit inspired the writer of Acts to say, "Peter, standing together with the eleven" (2:14). This indicates that Matthias, who was chosen in 1:26, was recognized as one among the twelve apostles.

Furthermore, there are other apostles in addition to the first twelve apostles. Barnabas was an apostle (Acts 14:14). Silas and Timothy also became apostles (1 Thes. 1:1; 2:6). In Revelation 2 the church in Ephesus was commended by the Lord because they discerned the genuine apostles from the false apostles (v. 2). This implies that there were more apostles than the twelve apostles; otherwise, it would have been easy to identify the false apostles.

Apostle is an anglicized Greek word which means one who is sent. Every proper believer is a sent one. There are examples of sent ones in the Old Testament. Isaiah was such a sent one. When he saw the glory of Christ (John 12:38, 41) and heard the voice of the Lord saying, "Whom shall I send? Who will go for us?" Isaiah said, "Here am I; send me" (Isa. 6:8). Whoever is sent by the Lord is an apostle. A little sister who is willing to be sent by the Lord to preach the gospel to her parents is an apostle, a sent one.

In the Lord's new way, we have been instructed, encouraged, and charged to go out to preach the gospel. Going out to preach the gospel equals being sent. As you go out to preach the gospel, you must have the realization that you are being sent. You should be able to declare to the Lord, "My going out is Your sending." Because everyone who goes out to preach the gospel is a sent one, the number of apostles is unlimited. To be sent out by the Lord is the intrinsic significance of the word *apostle*. Each day, if we would answer the Lord's call by saying, "Here am I, send me," we would be the Lord's sent ones, His apostles.

The stewardship mentioned in Ephesians 3:2 was given not only to Paul but also to all of the believers. Paul was a person fully consecrated to Christ, only caring for Christ day and night. The saints who have full-time jobs are a little different from Paul in that they must be occupied in making a living. In addition to this, there are various other affairs they have to take care of in regard to their families; otherwise, they could not survive. But even with such responsibilities, at least three hours could be spared during the week for the Lord's sake. You may tell the Lord, "Lord, I cannot be Your apostle with all of my time because I must earn a living. But I want to give You three hours a week. During these three hours, I would visit sinners with the gospel, feed the new believers, or perfect the saints." If you would do this, you would be an apostle of Christ during those three hours.

If we would be faithful with our time and dedicate three hours each week for the sake of the gospel, we would at least be genuine apostles during those three hours. You may be a salesman for a large company during your normal work hours, but when you go out to preach the gospel for the three hours which have been dedicated to the Lord, you are no longer a salesman, but an apostle fulfilling your stewardship to dispense Christ into people. As you go out to knock on doors, there is no need to tremble before men. You have received a glorious commission to dispense, distribute, and minister the glorious Christ into people. If someone should ask what you are doing, you could reply, "I am distributing the glorious Christ!"

In the full-time training in Anaheim, I trained the trainees not to preach the gospel according to the natural way. I instructed them not to ask questions of those to whom they are preaching the gospel. Rather, I encouraged them to speak in a bold way. We may say, "I have come to dispense Christ into you. He is glorious. He has sent me here to tell you that you must believe in Him. If you believe in Him, you will receive eternal life. Let's pray." If the person responds by saying, "I do not know how to pray," we can say, "Please, pray after me: 'Lord Jesus, I love You. Lord Jesus, I receive You. You are my Savior and life. Hallelujah! Lord Jesus. Amen.'" After a person has prayed to receive the Lord, he should then be directed to be baptized. This also should not be in the way of asking whether or not the person would like to be baptized. Rather, the person should just be led to be baptized. To ask questions either at the time of prayer or at the time of baptism is unwise. To preach the gospel in the way of authority is to be a proper sent one, an apostle.

Paul received the stewardship through the grace given to him. We also have been given grace to take the God-ordained way. Before going out we should pray, "Lord Jesus, thank You that You have given us a commission to go out with Your authority to minister Yourself to sinners. Lord, go with us." When you go out in this way, you go full of power and authority. This authority may be likened to that of a policeman. The policeman who directs traffic seems to be just a small man with a uniform standing in the middle of the street. However, a car which is more powerful than the policeman must stop at his command. The car has power but the man has authority. The policeman has the authority because the government is behind him supporting him. We must obey him, or we risk receiving a fine. When we go out to preach the gospel, we also must realize that the entire divine government is behind us. We go out in the powerful name of the Lord Jesus. When we go to visit people in the homes and tell them that we have come in the name of Jesus, Satan trembles. Satan and the evil angels must retreat, because the name of Jesus is full of authority.

To preach the gospel according to the New Testament is to distribute Christ in His authority. You receive the authority by your prayer to the Lord before going out. In your going, God operates by distributing to you the sufficient grace as your capital to carry out the preaching of the gospel. In this way, you go out with the power, authority, and position as one of the apostles of Christ. You have the stewardship and the commission. In Matthew 28:18-19 the Lord said, "All authority has been given to Me in heaven and on earth. Go therefore and disciple all the nations." The Lord Jesus has received all authority and He has charged us to go. Our problem is that we often do not act on what the Lord has given us. The Lord as the Head of the Body has given all of the members of His Body authority to disciple the nations. We must assume this authority and go. We are apostles to those whom we baptize. Because Paul was the one who initially brought the gospel to the Corinthians, he could say,

"If to others I am not an apostle, yet surely I am to you; for you are the seal of my apostleship in the Lord" (1 Cor. 9:2). We also are apostles to those whom we lead to believe and be baptized.

THE APOSTLE'S STEWARDSHIP
DISPENSING THE RICHES OF CHRIST

The Stewardship of the Grace of God Given to the Apostle

The apostle's stewardship was for dispensing the riches of Christ (Eph. 3:2-5, 7-11). The stewardship of the grace of God was given not only to the apostle Paul (Eph. 3:2) but to all of us as well. This stewardship was given by revelation concerning the church as the mystery of Christ, which was not made known to men in other generations (vv. 3-5). The revelation of the mystery makes the apostle a minister, with the grace of God dispensed into him, to minister to the nations the unsearchable riches of Christ through the dispensing of the rich Christ (vv. 7-8). When we go out to visit people with the gospel, we go out to minister Christ with His unsearchable riches to sinners. We do not go to minister doctrine, philosophy, logic, or religion. Rather, we go to minister the unsearchable riches of Christ directly into people. We do this in much the same way as a waiter or steward serves a meal to the patrons of a restaurant. A waiter would not just come to the patrons and describe how clean the restaurant is, how qualified the cook is, or how the food is being cooked. If he would do this, those waiting for their food would grow very impatient. Our preaching of the gospel in the past was very often just like this. We gave a lot of explanation, doctrine, and teaching to people, but very little Christ. Therefore, the response was usually not very positive. We must learn to minister the rich Christ to people directly.

The stewardship of the grace of God was given to the apostle to bring to light the economy of the mystery, which from the ages had been hidden in God, who created all things (v. 9). The mystery is no longer hidden; it is an open fact today.

The Stewardship of the Grace of God
Being for the Constituting of the Church

The stewardship of the grace of God is for the constituting of the church, through the dispensing of the unsearchable riches of Christ, to make the multifarious wisdom of God known to the rulers and the authorities in the heavenlies, according to God's eternal purpose made in Christ (Eph. 3:10-11). When you go out for three hours a week to minister the riches of Christ into sinners, you must realize that the result will be that the church is constituted. It is a shame to us that many of the churches have existed in many cities for a number of years, yet the number of saints is still relatively small. How could a local church be built up with only a small number year after year? In order to build a house, there is the need of material. You cannot build a great house with a little material. In Haggai the Lord charged the children of Israel to go up to the mountain to bring wood in order to build His house (1:8). We must go out to disciple the nations in order to make them members of the Body of Christ. By the increase of the material, there will be something with which to build the church. This is the stewardship which was given not only to Paul but also to the entire Body when the Lord charged the disciples after His resurrection in Matthew 28:18-19.

CHRIST MAKING HIS HOME
IN THE HEARTS OF THE SAINTS

Through the dispensing of the riches of Christ, Christ is ministered into sinners. He is no longer outside of His believers; He is now inside of them. The Christ who was crucified on the cross now lives in us. Christ has been ministered into us, so we now have Christ making His home in our hearts (Eph. 3:16-17). Since we have received Christ, He is working and moving within us. He is working and moving in the heavens, in the church, and in our environment, but His main work is to work Himself into us, to make home in our hearts, to get Himself settled down within us.

The Lord desires to settle Himself down within us, but we

often keep Him within a small part of our being. When I travel to different cities, I often stay as a guest in the homes of the saints. Since I am a guest, I do not settle down by unpacking my suitcase completely. On the contrary, I leave my suitcase partially packed because I know that after a few days I will leave again and have to repack everything. I also realize that as a guest it is inappropriate for me to touch things within the saints' homes unless I have been given permission to do so. As a guest, I am restricted in my activity. This illustrates how the Lord Jesus is often restricted within us. The Lord Jesus is often like a guest within us. He may have been living within us for fifteen years, but He may still not yet be "unpacked." He also may not dare to do things within us because we have not given Him the permission to do so. He may still be restricted to our spirit, unable to occupy the rest of our inner being.

Our being may be likened to a house with many rooms. The Lord may be limited to the "living room" of our inner being. Because the Lord is limited to the living room, it may have become a little prison to Him. We have other rooms in our being, but they are secret rooms because we have not allowed the Lord to enter these rooms. These rooms include our mind, emotion, will, and conscience. We love the Lord Jesus, but we may not have given Him any ground in our emotion. This may also be the case with our mind. In the way we live, in the way we dress ourselves, and in the way we drive our car, there may be no ground for Christ. In the same way, many of our decisions may have been made without any ground given to Christ. We may be the only one occupying our mind, will, emotion, and conscience. As a result, Christ has been a guest within us and even a prisoner within us.

Paul first told the saints at Ephesus that he was a steward with a commission to distribute, to minister, the riches of Christ into the believers (3:2, 8). But in carrying out this stewardship, he realized that Christ was not yet settled down within them. Christ was dwelling in their spirit, but He had not yet settled down in their heart. Christ was in the center of the saints' being, in their spirit, but He had not yet come into the parts of their soul surrounding their spirit. The parts of the soul include the mind, emotion, and will. These parts of the soul with the conscience of the spirit form the heart. Christ was limited and imprisoned within their spirit; He could not spread into the inner parts of their being. This is the reason that Paul prayed for Christ to make His home in the hearts of the saints. For Christ to make His home in our hearts means that He is able to spread Himself into our mind, emotion, will, and conscience. In this way Christ will occupy our entire inner being. Thus, Christ will become settled in our being, and our inner being will become His home.

Through the Father's Strengthening of the Saints into Their Inner Man with the Dispensing of the Riches of the Father's Glory

The operation of the Divine Trinity is needed for Christ to make home in our hearts. It is for this reason that Paul prayed to the Father as the source that He would strengthen the saints into their inner man with the dispensing of the riches of the Father's glory (Eph. 3:16). The Father's glory is the Father's splendor. Splendor refers to the outward expression of something. If you are a proper person, you will have human virtues such as wisdom, knowledge, and love. If you are such a person, you will have a certain kind of expression. This expression is your splendor, your glory. The glory of God is just the expression of what God is in all of His divine attributes. These attributes include love, light, power, patience, and mercy. The expression of God in His attributes is His splendor.

Through the Spirit's Operating within the Saints with the Dispensing of the Divine Power

Christ makes His home in the hearts of the saints through the Spirit's operating within the saints with the dispensing of the divine power (Eph. 3:16). The Spirit is within us as the power of God. Just as power can be a synonym for electricity, the Spirit is a synonym for the power of God. Today many Christians lack this proper knowledge. They may know that the Spirit is within them, but they do not realize that this Spirit is not only their life but also their power. The power has been installed. Our need is to "switch on" the Spirit. The Spirit will then operate within us with the dispensing of the divine power.

That Christ May Make His Home in the Saints' Hearts

Christ makes His home in the hearts of the saints through the operation of the Triune God (Eph. 3:17a). The Father strengthens us according to the riches of what He is, the Spirit operates in power, and the Son makes His home in our hearts. With the Father's strengthening and the Spirit's empowering, the Son has the ground, the opportunity, to enlarge Himself in our inner being. He enlarges Himself in our being by penetrating into our mind, spreading into our will, occupying our emotion, and taking over our entire conscience. In this way Christ occupies our entire inner being, making home in all of our heart. This takes place by the dispensing of Himself into all the parts of our heart.

Having Been Rooted and Grounded in Love

As Christ is making home in our hearts, we are being rooted and grounded in love (Eph. 3:17b). We are God's farm and God's building (1 Cor. 3:9). As God's farm we need to be rooted for growth, and as God's building we need to be grounded for building up. Being rooted and grounded is in love. To experience Christ, we need faith and love (1 Tim. 1:14). Faith enables us to realize Christ, and love enables us to enjoy Him. Both faith and love are not ours but His. His faith becomes our faith to believe in Him, and His love becomes our love to love Him.

Being Strong to Apprehend with All the Saints the Dimensions of Christ

Christ making His home in our hearts enables us to apprehend with all the saints the dimensions of Christ— the breadth, length, height, and depth (Eph. 3:18). Christ is unsearchable, untraceable, unlimited, all-inclusive, and all-extensive. He is the breadth, length, height, and depth. These are the dimensions of the universe. No one can say how broad the breadth is, how long the length is, how high the height is, or how deep the depth is. All of these dimensions are Christ. As we allow Christ to get settled in our inner parts through the dispensing of His riches into us, gradually we will realize with all the saints that the Christ we enjoy is unsearchable, unlimited, all-inclusive, and all-extensive. We will apprehend with all the saints His breadth, length, height, and depth.

Knowing the Knowledge-surpassing Love of Christ

Christ making His home in our hearts causes us to know the knowledge-surpassing love of Christ (Eph. 3:19a). To know the knowledge-surpassing love of Christ is to realize that Christ is everything to us. Christ is our breath, our rest, our daily life, and our home. He is also our drink, our food, our clothing, our wisdom, our knowledge, our sanctification, and our redemption. He is everything! As a result, His love is knowledge-surpassing.

Being Filled unto All the Fullness of God for the Corporate Expression of the Processed Triune God

When Christ is fully settled down within our hearts, we, the saints, are filled with the dispensing of the unsearchable riches of the all-inclusive Christ as the embodiment of the Triune God unto all the fullness of God for the corporate expression of the processed Triune God (Eph. 3:19b). This means that what God is becomes what we are. We are filled with the dispensing of the unsearchable riches of Christ as the embodiment of the Triune God to such an extent that we are filled unto all the fullness of the Triune God. This fullness is the expression of God, and this expression is the Body of Christ, the organism of the Triune God.

Our eyes need to be enlightened to see the church according to God's high standard. Much of today's speaking about the church is too low. We need a vision to uplift our view and to rescue us from a low understanding concerning the church.

We make mistakes which devastate the practical church life because our understanding is too low. We need to be rescued. This rescue comes from a proper view and an uplifted vision concerning the church, the Body of Christ, the organism of the Triune God.

CHAPTER THREE

THE DIVINE DISPENSING
OF THE DIVINE TRINITY
FOR THE BUILDING UP OF
THE ORGANIC BODY OF CHRIST

Scripture Reading: Eph. 4:4-16

We have seen that the divine dispensing through the Father's choosing and predestinating, through the Son's redeeming, and through the Spirit's sealing causes us to have the Father's holy nature and divine life. Through the Father's holy nature and divine life with the Son's divine element, we are constituted into a treasure which the Father can inherit. We become the Father's inheritance through the Son's redeeming us into His divine element. Ultimately, we also receive the Spirit's sealing through the divine dispensing. The Holy Spirit as the consummation of the Triune God is the sealing ink which continually seals us throughout our entire Christian life until the day of the redemption of our body (Eph. 1:14). The holy nature, the divine life, the divine inheritance as the issue of Christ's divine element, and the sealing ink issue in the organic Body of Christ.

THE DIVINE DISPENSING IN THE GOSPEL OF JOHN

The Gospel of John is a book concerning the divine dispensing. The first point of God's dispensing introduced in the Gospel of John is incarnation. The most crucial verse in chapter one is verse 14, which says, "And the Word became flesh...." From my youth, I was told that the subject of the Gospel of John is Christ as the divine person, and that this book presents Christ as the very God. This is because the gospel is a matter of receiving the divine life, which is Christ Himself. Christ became the embodiment of the divine life

(John 1:4) through incarnation. Though I had received this teaching sixty years ago, I did not have the deep impression that the incarnation was the first step of God's dispensing. Now I realize that incarnation was for God to dispense Himself into man. Man was created by God in His image with the definite purpose of being one with God.

God Being Good for Food

The oneness that God desires with man is illustrated by what takes place when we eat, digest, and assimilate food. When you eat a sandwich, your stomach works to digest and assimilate the contents of that sandwich. Another word for this process is dispensing. Digestion and assimilation are dispensing. After a few hours, the sandwich disappears within you to become one with you. Eventually, the sandwich is mingled with you. This is the kind of oneness God desires to have with man. To obtain this oneness God has made Himself edible. He is the bread of life (John 6:35, 57). The first stanza and chorus of hymn #1145 in *Hymns* say:

> God gave His Son to man to be
> The tree of life so rich and free,
> That every man may taste and see
> That God is good for food.

> Yes, God is good for food!
> Yes, God is good for food!
> We've tasted and we testify
> That God is good for food!

Our God is good for food. He is not only good for salvation and redemption; He is also good for food. In John 6:51 Jesus said, "I am the living bread which came down out of heaven; if anyone eats of this bread, he shall live forever." In the wilderness the children of Israel ate manna every day (Exo. 16:14-15, 21). They lived on that supply of manna for forty years. In the Gospel of John, the Lord Jesus revealed Himself as the real manna. He should not be eaten only once a year but every day. Jesus is our daily manna. We must eat Him every day.

We need to eat Him every day, and we need to be revived by Him each day. In the ancient time, the Israelites had to collect the manna before the rising of the sun, because when the sun became hot, the manna melted (Exo. 16:21). It is the same with our practice of morning revival. We must rise up early. If you are lazy and like to sleep late in the morning, you will miss the manna. You need to rise earlier, before the rising of the sun, in order to pick up Christ as your daily manna. You must eat Christ. This is the divine thought in the divine Word.

The Process of the Divine Dispensing

According to the Gospel of John, the eternal God who created the heavens and the earth became a man. The process whereby He became a man was by entering the womb of a virgin, Mary. He was the great God who created the heavens and the earth, but He came into a virgin's womb and remained there for nine months until His birth. The Word which was God became flesh in the way ordained by God for every man's birth. He came by way of conception and birth. He was born as a little babe named Jesus. The shepherds in the fields around Bethlehem came to see the baby wrapped in cloths and lying in a manger (Luke 2:12, 15-16). As a babe, He escaped to Egypt and returned to a village called Nazareth in the despised region of Galilee (Matt. 2:13-14, 19-23). He lived in Nazareth for thirty years and worked as a carpenter. At the age of thirty, the age according to God's ordination that a man may enter into the service of the tabernacle (Num. 4:46-47), the Lord Jesus came out to preach, but He actually came out to dispense. He did not dispense doctrine. He began to dispense Himself as the God-man. As He began to dispense Himself, people were attracted.

When I was young, I could not understand why the Lord Jesus was so attractive. Peter, Andrew, James, and John dropped everything to follow Him (Matt. 4:18-22). He was like an immense magnet, drawing His seekers to Himself. He attracted all kinds of men and women, even a wife of a high official (Luke 8:3). Many followed Him during the three and a half years of His ministry because He infused the embodied

God into people. Many in Christianity hold the concept that the Lord was merely teaching His disciples during this time, but this understanding is too shallow. It was not a matter of the disciples receiving some doctrine or teaching. They received a living person. This person was dispensed into them.

God's incarnation was the first step of the divine dispensing. His human living was the second step, and His death was the third step. After the three and a half years of His ministry, the Lord Jesus went to the cross and died in order to accomplish an all-inclusive death. The main purpose of His death was not to take away sins, but to release the divine life. He was a grain of wheat falling into the ground to die (John 12:24). A grain of wheat remains the same until it is sown into soil. In the soil it dies, and through death the inner life within the grain is released. The main aspect of Christ's all-inclusive death was the release of His divine life. The release of the divine life is the dispensing of the divine life.

After passing through death, the Lord Jesus entered into resurrection. His death released the divine life, and His resurrection applied the divine life. In resurrection He regenerated us (1 Pet. 1:3). We were regenerated two thousand years ago, before our natural birth. Our regeneration preceded our natural birth. Many count our regeneration as our second birth. This is correct, but we must also realize that our second birth took place before our first birth. According to our experience we were first born physically, and then spiritually. But in God's sight, we were regenerated two thousand years ago at the resurrection of Christ. We know this because the Bible tells us so in 1 Peter 1:3.

Through incarnation, human living, death, and resurrection with regeneration, the processed Triune God is now within us. His being in us is not a small thing. He is no longer in the manger, on the cross, in the tomb, or in Hades. He is not just in the heavens; He is in us. If He were only in the heavens, He would be apart from and far away from us, but He is now with us and in us. He is nearer and dearer to us than anyone. Our wife or husband can be with us, but they can never get into us. Jesus is within us all the time. We are so small, yet the processed and consummated Triune God dwells within us.

In resurrection, the Lord became the life-giving Spirit (1 Cor. 15:45b). On the evening of the day of His resurrection, He came back to His disciples and said to them, "Receive the Holy Spirit" (John 20:22). The Holy Spirit here was the holy breath as the processed and consummated Triune God. In eternity He was the Word. He then was conceived in the womb and born as a little babe in a manger. He lived as a man in Nazareth. He began to travel and minister. Eventually, He went to the cross, to the tomb, and to Hades. He then entered into resurrection. In resurrection He became the Spirit to regenerate us. After regenerating us, He stays within us. This wonderful One who was the Word in the beginning is now within us. He is within us as the all-inclusive, life-giving Spirit, who is the consummated, processed Triune God.

In John 7:37-38 the Lord Jesus told us that He is the living water for us to drink, and in John 6:35 He said that He is the bread of life for us to eat. The intrinsic view of the Gospel of John concerning the Triune God is that He went through all of the processes to be consummated so that He could be available for His chosen people to eat, drink, and breathe. Now He is within all of His eaters, drinkers, and breathers.

Growing with the Increase of God

The work of assimilation is a good illustration of dispensing. Immediately after eating, the fine work of dispensing begins in order to dispense the food into the cells, fibers, and tissues of our being. In the same way, the dispensing of the Triune God is to make the processed and consummated Triune God the very constitution of our being. This fine work of dispensing continues day by day and will be finalized when the sealing ink of the Spirit permeates through our entire body (Eph. 1:13-14). This will be the redemption of our body (Rom. 8:23) when we are glorified.

The dispensing of the Triune God into us causes us to grow with the increase of God (Col. 2:19). For anything to grow it must increase with some element or substance. Human beings grow by the food they take in. If you do not eat anything, you cannot grow. We Christians grow with the increase, the surplus, the addition, of God. God entered into us when we were regenerated. Now He is increasing within us by adding more of Himself to us. However, the amount of God each brother or sister has differs.

To have the Lord increase within us, we must come to the Word of God to eat each day. The first stanza of *Hymns*, #811 shows how we must come to the Lord to be fed by Him:

> My heart is hungry, my spirit doth thirst;
> I come to Thee, Lord, to seek Thy supply;
> All that I need is none other but Thee,
> Thou canst my hunger and thirst satisfy.

> Feed me, Lord Jesus, give me to drink,
> Fill all my hunger, quench all my thirst;
> Flood me with joy, be the strength of my life,
> Fill all my hunger, quench all my thirst.

We also must pray in order to be fed by the Lord. Many times, I do not have the time to close my door, kneel down, and pray, but I can say that I often have a spirit of prayer. I have a kind of aspiration within me, and this aspiration causes me to breathe the Lord in very much. It causes me to inhale the living, processed, consummated God into my being.

THE DIVINE DISPENSING OF THE DIVINE TRINITY

One Body with One Spirit Dispensing Himself to the Body as the Spiritual Essence of the Body, Bringing in the Hope of Glory to the Body

Ephesians 4:4-6 reveals the dispensing of the Divine Trinity. Verse 4 says that there is one Body and one Spirit. The one Spirit in this verse is the processed, consummated God, the pneumatic Christ. This Spirit is just Christ Himself. We can illustrate this by the way a big melon is processed to become juice. First, there is a big melon which is cut into slices. Then the slices are pressed until juice is produced. The juice is the "spirit" of the melon. The juice of the melon is actually the melon itself. In the same way, the Spirit is the "sliced and pressed Jesus." The Spirit in the Body of Christ is Christ after He was "cut" on the cross and "pressed" unto death. Now in resurrection, He is the Spirit, the "juice." Through His death and resurrection, He has become the drinkable Spirit. Our need is to drink Him. He is within us, but every day we need more of Him. Although we drink today, it does not mean that one drink will be sufficient for our entire life. Our drinking should be continuous. In eternity, we will still need to drink the river of the water of life (Rev. 22:1, 17) and eat the tree of life (v. 14). We need to eat and drink for eternity.

Ephesians 4:4 says that there is one Body and one Spirit, and verse 5 says, "One Lord, one faith, one baptism." Apparently, the one Spirit is different from the one Lord. They seem to be two. Actually, They are one. If you drink the juice of a melon, you have the melon. The "juice" of Christ is the Spirit. When you drink the Spirit, you drink the Lord. Second Corinthians 3:17 says, "And the Lord is the Spirit," and verse 18 says that as we are beholding and reflecting the glory of the Lord, we are transformed into the same image "even as from the Lord Spirit." The "Lord Spirit" is a compound title which indicates that the Spirit is the Lord. Whenever we experience the Spirit, we feel that we are being governed, but when we are free from the Spirit, we become wild, uncontrollable, and unrestrained. The Spirit is the Lord.

One Lord Dispensing Himself to the Body as the Divine Element of the Body through the Uniting Faith and the Separating Baptism of the Members of the Body

Ephesians 4:5 says, "One Lord, one faith, one baptism." We know what both faith and baptism are. But when these two things are put together with the one Lord, they are more difficult to understand. After much seeking of the Lord, I began to realize that faith always goes along with the Lord. We do not have faith of ourselves. Jesus is faith. If you have Jesus, you have faith. He is the Originator, the Author, and the Finisher, the Perfecter, of faith (Heb. 12:2). This faith unites us to the Lord. When you appreciate the Lord, worship Him, esteem Him, and go along with Him, immediately faith is with you, uniting you to the Lord.

Baptism goes along with faith. Faith unites us to the positive things, and baptism separates us from the negative things. When we were baptized, we were separated from the world. We also must realize that the uniting of faith and the separation of baptism are lifelong matters. Every day, when we esteem the Lord, we have the deep sensation that faith is within us uniting us to Him. In the same way and at the same time, baptism is separating us from all the negative things. Baptism in our daily life is our realization and application of the death of Christ. The realization and application of the death of Christ separates us from our temper, the world, sin, the self, our natural life, and everything that is negative. This separation is the application of Christ's death. In 2 Corinthians 4:12 Paul said, "So then death operates in us, but life in you," and in verse 10 Paul calls the death of Christ "the putting to death of Jesus." The death which operates in us and the putting to death of Jesus are the realization and application of the death of Christ in our daily life. Thus, baptism separates us from all of the negative things.

One God as the Father of All, Who Is over All as the Father, through All as the Son, and in All as the Spirit, Dispensing the Fullness of His Divine Trinity to All the Members of the Body

Ultimately, in Ephesians 4:6 there is "one God and Father of all, who is over all and through all and in all." God the Father is in three situations: He is over all, through all, and in all. "Over all" indicates that He is the overshadowing One, covering us and taking care of us all the time. "Through all" means that He knows our situation intimately because He has passed through all of the things regarding us. If you are a manager of a company, you must go through all of the offices and rooms of your company in order to know what is going on. "In all" means that He stays within us. Thus, the Triune God is in three situations. "Over all" refers to the Father, "through all" refers to the Son, and "in all" refers to the Spirit. The Father functions as the Father, the Son, and the Spirit. Eventually, this One is the Triune God. The Father is the source, the Son is the course, and the Spirit is the flow. These Three are one in reaching us.

The divine dispensing comes out of the Three of the Divine Trinity—the Father, the Son, and the Spirit. The divine dispensing taking place within us is the operating of the all-inclusive, life-giving Spirit, the pneumatic Christ, as the aggregate, totality, and consummation of the Triune God. This Spirit is moving in us, anointing us, watering us, feeding us, satisfying us, strengthening us, comforting us, saturating us, and permeating us. There are so many words to describe His dispensing within us. All of the foregoing items, such as watering, feeding, strengthening, permeating, saturating, and anointing, are matters of dispensing. Every day we should be built up by receiving the divine dispensing within us.

We should not expect to have a spectacular time each day in receiving the divine dispensing. I recently spoke a word to the trainees in the full-time training concerning their daily spiritual life. I told them not to expect to have a spectacular result in their Christian life. We should forget about having something spectacular. We must learn to be satisfied with ordinary days which are filled with regular and normal practices in the divine dispensing. In the morning we should have some time with the Lord to touch Him and be revived by Him. Then we need to pass through a daily routine to get ready for work. To live a life in the divine dispensing in a normal way will make us healthy both physically and spiritually. Whether or not we have good or bad days is not up to us; it is up to His sovereignty. He has already chosen us, and it is too late to turn back. We are blessed because the processed and consummated Triune God is within us. He is in us, not in a spectacular way but in a very ordinary way.

We should be blessed to be satisfied with ordinary days in the divine dispensing. The Triune God is certainly in us, but

His being in us is not spectacular. Every day He is within us dispensing and positively strengthening and encouraging us. In the last three years, I have experienced many troubles, yet nothing has disturbed me. I have published more messages, I have visited more places, and I have held more conferences. However, this is not because I have had spectacular days. I have just lived an ordinary life of receiving His dispensing. The Epistles reveal that the work of Christ within us is a fine work of dispensing. I cannot tell you how much the fine dispensing has been going on within me during these last three years. Our destiny is to live an ordinary life in the divine dispensing. Our Father God has destined that we live in an ordinary way under His continual dispensing.

FOR THE BUILDING UP
OF THE ORGANIC BODY OF CHRIST

By Christ, the Head of the Body,
Constituting the Members of the Body into Gifts
through the Dispensing of the Riches
in His Resurrection and Ascension

The divine dispensing of the Divine Trinity is for the building up of the Body of Christ (Eph. 4:7-16). Through this divine dispensing, gifts have been constituted by Christ as the crucified, resurrected, and ascended Head. As the Head of the Body, Christ constituted the members of the Body into gifts through the dispensing of the riches in His resurrection and ascension (vv. 7-10).

By Christ, as the Head of the Body
in His Ascension, Giving Some Apostles,
Some Prophets, Some Evangelists, and
Some Shepherds and Teachers
as Gifts to His Body,
to Dispense to His Body
All That He Is, Has, and Has Attained

The particular gifts He gave to the church were some apostles, some prophets, some evangelists, and some shepherds and teachers (v. 11). These gifts do a perfecting work until all the saints in the Body are perfected. All the saints will be perfected to do the work of apostles, prophets, evangelists, and shepherds and teachers. The professors in a college make their students the same as they are after a period of years. At the beginning the students who enter the college are merely students. But eventually, they can become professors with the ability to teach. In Christianity the perfecting by the gifts, which corresponds to the teaching of the professors in a college, is not that widespread. We also must admit that we have lacked this kind of perfecting in the past. This is the reason that we need to change our practice from the old way to the new way. The new way is a way in which all the gifted persons perfect the other members of the Body of Christ to do what they do. In this way all of the saints will be perfected.

The perfecting of the saints by the gifts is for the work of the New Testament ministry, for the building up of the Body of Christ through the dispensing of the riches of Christ (v. 12). This perfecting is so that all the members may arrive at the oneness of the faith and of the full knowledge of the Son of God, at a full-grown man, and at the measure of the stature of the fullness of Christ (v. 13). Perfecting is a matter of dispensing. Thus, the new way is a matter of dispensing. It is not merely to teach.

In the new way of group meetings, we do not like to assign a teacher or leader to any group. We just encourage the saints to come together. If someone has a problem, we encourage the saints to fellowship, to pray for each other, to help each other, to care for each other, and to shepherd each other. There are no assigned teachers or students. Everyone can ask, everyone can answer, everyone can teach, and everyone can learn. This issues in the perfecting of the saints to function for the building up of the Body of Christ.

By the Members of the Body Holding to Truth in Love That They May Grow Up into the Head, Christ, in All Things

Ephesians 4:15 says, "But holding to truth in love, we may grow up into Him in all things, who is the Head, Christ."

Because all the riches of the Head have been dispensed into us, we grow with these riches in all things into the Head. Then out from the Head all the Body, joined closely together through every joint of the rich supply and knit together (interwoven) through the operation of each part in its measure, causes the growth of the Body, through the dispensing of the riches of the processed Triune God, unto the organic building up of the Body itself in love (v. 16).

In Ephesians 4:16 there are two groups of believers or members. One group is the joints of the rich supply. These joints supply the Body. The second group includes the parts which function in their measure. Through these two groups, the Body is joined closely together and knit together. In a physical building of stones, there is also the joining and the knitting. The frames of the building need to be joined together. This corresponds to the work of the joints of the rich supply, who join together the members. Once the building is framed, the gaps are filled by interweaving pieces of stone between the frames. This is the knitting together. Eventually, all the parts of the building are made one. The Body of Christ is the organic building, the organism of the Triune God. By the joining closely together and knitting together, this organic building will not only be one but will also cause its own growth unto the building up of itself in love.

The intrinsic concept of verse 16 is the dispensing of the Triune God. This dispensing is through the Head, through the gifted persons, and through the perfected ones, that the Body may be built up. First, the Head initiates the dispensing to the gifted persons. Then this dispensing goes through the gifted persons to the perfected ones. Then the perfected ones, the functioning ones, will dispense to others. It is by this thorough step-by-step dispensing that the Body grows and builds itself up. This is the dispensing of the consummated Triune God, the pneumatic Christ as the life-giving Spirit. He is anointing, moving, feeding, nourishing, strengthening, comforting, encouraging, and working within us. Every day we have to come back to the Spirit and remain in Him all the time. We must be one with the moving One within us. Then we will experience His fine work of divine dispensing. The work of the divine dispensing will not be finalized until our body is saturated and permeated by the sealing Spirit to be glorified.

CHAPTER FOUR

THE DIVINE DISPENSING OF THE DIVINE TRINITY AS THE DIVINE LIFE

Scripture Reading: John 1:14; 3:16; 12:24; 19:34; 3:5; 1 Pet. 1:3b; John 20:22; 4:14; 6:56-58a; 14:9-11, 16-20; 7:38-39; 15:5, 16a; 21:15, 17

In this chapter we shall consider the divine dispensing of the Divine Trinity as the divine life. The Divine Trinity is God Himself in His divine person, the divine life is the life of God, and the divine dispensing is the Triune God's dispensing of Himself into us as our life.

The Gospel of John is a Gospel of the divine life. It presents the divine life not in an objective way but in a subjective way. It gives us a particular and wonderful picture of how God came to be a man in order to dispense Himself into man that man may receive Him and enjoy Him as his inner life. According to His divine economy, God's intention was to be one with man. God's desire to be one with man is illustrated in the Bible by eating. Both the Old Testament and the New Testament show us that God is our food. After God created man, He put him in front of the tree of life (Gen. 2:9, 16-17), indicating that God wanted man to eat of Him and take Him as his life, causing man to become one with Him. The food that we eat is digested and assimilated into us, becoming the constituent of our very being. In the same way, God wanted man to take Him as his food that He might be man's constituent.

THE INCARNATION OF THE DIVINE TRINITY, DISPENSING THE DIVINE GRACE AND REALITY TO MEN

In order to carry out His intention, God first became incarnated. Before the incarnation, God was only God, separate from the man created by Him. For God to be incarnated means that He became a man with a human body of blood and flesh (Heb. 2:14). The incarnation of the Divine Trinity dispensed the divine grace and reality to men. John 1:14 says, "And the Word became flesh and tabernacled among us (and we beheld His glory, glory as of an only begotten from a father), full of grace and reality." According to the teaching of the New Testament, grace is God Himself given to us for our enjoyment. Grace is not something outward, such as a good house, a good car, or a good business. In 1 Corinthians 15:10 Paul indicated that grace is a person, saying, "I labored more abundantly than all of them, yet not I, but the grace of God with me." Grace is God Himself to be received and enjoyed by man.

Reality in John 1:14 is the very God whom we touch, gain, and possess. Nothing is as real as God. Other than God, everything is vanity of vanities (Eccl. 1:2). When we receive God, we have the reality. Both grace and reality are God Himself. God became flesh in order to dispense Himself into us. When He is dispensed into us, He is the grace we enjoy, and He is the reality we possess. The purpose of God's incarnation was for God to dispense Himself to us as grace and reality.

THE GIVING OF GOD'S
ONLY BEGOTTEN SON TO THE WORLD,
DISPENSING THE DIVINE LIFE TO MEN

John 3:16 says, "For God so loved the world that He gave His only begotten Son, that everyone who believes in Him should not perish, but have eternal life." The giving of God's only begotten Son to the world dispensed the divine life to men. God gave His Son to us not only that we may be saved through the Son, but even the more that He could dispense Himself into us. According to the Gospel of John, when the Son comes, He comes with the Father (8:29). Therefore, when the Father gave the Son to us, He gave Himself with the Son. When we receive the Son, we receive the Father. The giving of the Son of God to us is a matter of the divine dispensing.

THE DEATH OF THE INCARNATED SON,
RELEASING THE DIVINE LIFE WITHIN HIM
FOR THE DIVINE DISPENSING

The death of Christ on the cross was also a part of the divine dispensing. The death of the incarnated Son released the divine life within Him for the divine dispensing (John 12:24; 19:34). John 12:24 says, "Truly, truly, I say to you, unless a grain of wheat falls into the ground and dies, it abides alone; but if it dies, it bears much fruit." Within the shell of a grain of wheat is the life of the wheat. For the grain of wheat to die is to release the life within its shell. The life within the shell cannot be released until the shell is broken, and when it is broken, the life within is released to produce many grains. First, it is one grain alone; then it becomes many grains. This is the dispensing of the inner life of the one grain into the many grains. Jesus as the grain of wheat was the divine seed. The divine life was concealed in His "shell." When Jesus went to the cross and was put to death, He broke through the shell to release His inner life, the divine life, into His many believers, the many grains.

THE RESURRECTION OF THE CRUCIFIED SON,
IMPARTING THE DIVINE LIFE
INTO THE REGENERATED BELIEVERS
FOR THE DIVINE DISPENSING

First, God was incarnated to be a man, and God gave Himself in the Son to man that man may receive Him. Then, in order to be man's life, He went through death to release the divine life within Him. After His crucifixion, Christ resurrected from the dead. The resurrection of the crucified Son imparted the divine life into the regenerated believers for the divine dispensing (John 3:5; 1 Pet. 1:3b). Christ's death released His divine life from within His human shell, and the resurrection imparted and applied the divine life to us. This application took place at the time we were regenerated. We were all born of the flesh, needing to be reborn of the Spirit. John 3:6 says, "That which is born of the flesh is flesh, and that which is born of the Spirit is spirit." In our second birth, our spirit was regenerated by the Spirit, who is Christ in resurrection. First Peter 1:3 says, "Blessed be the God and Father of our Lord Jesus Christ, who according to His great mercy has regenerated us unto a living hope through the resurrection of Jesus Christ from among the dead." According to our view, we were regenerated after we were born. However, according to God's view, we were regenerated when Christ was resurrected nearly two thousand years ago.

THE BREATHING OF THE PNEUMATIC CHRIST IN HIS RESURRECTION INTO THE DISCIPLES, DISPENSING THE CONSUMMATED SPIRIT AS THE CONSUMMATION OF THE PROCESSED TRIUNE GOD FOR THE DIVINE DISPENSING

In the incarnation God became a man, but in His resurrection, Christ as the last Adam, a man in the flesh, became a life-giving Spirit (1 Cor. 15:45). The breathing of the pneumatic Christ in His resurrection into the disciples dispensed the consummated Spirit as the consummation of the processed Triune God for the divine dispensing (John 20:22). Christ is rich and has many aspects. He was incarnated to be a man, and He was given to us. Then He died on the cross for us to solve the problem of sin, becoming our Redeemer. Then He resurrected and ascended to heaven to be our Savior. Moreover, He also became a life-giving Spirit to dwell in us. On the cross He was our Redeemer, in the heavens He is our Savior, and within us He is the life-giving Spirit to be our life.

On the evening of the day of His resurrection, He came back to His disciples in a secret and marvelous way. He came into the room where they were, breathed into them, and said, "Receive the Holy Spirit" (John 20:19-22). John 20 only tells us how Jesus came to the disciples. It does not tell us how He left again. It is difficult to discover where Jesus went after the evening of His resurrection. The Gospels of Mark and Luke tell us that after His resurrection Jesus ascended to the heavens, but there is no such record in the Gospel of John. After Jesus was resurrected, He simply came back to His disciples and breathed Himself into them as the holy breath.

From that time Jesus never left them. He was, still is, and will be forever in all His disciples.

THE PNEUMATIC CHRIST
FOR THE BELIEVERS' BREATHING,
THE LIVING WATER GIVEN
BY CHRIST IN RESURRECTION,
AND THE RESURRECTED CHRIST EATEN BY
THE BELIEVERS AND INDWELLING THEM

The Gospel of John has two lines concerning the divine dispensing. First, the wonderful Christ was God. Then He was incarnated and was given to us as the Son. Following this He died, resurrected, and became the life-giving Spirit to breathe Himself into His disciples. This is the first line. However, the Gospel of John has another line, showing us how Jesus is dispensed into us. In regeneration, Christ came into us and we were born again. However, after a child is born, he needs to breathe, drink, and eat. The pneumatic Christ is for the believer's breathing, dispensing the divine essence into them. The living water is given by Christ in resurrection, dispensing the divine riches into the believers (4:14). The resurrected Christ is eaten by the believers and indwells them, dispensing the divine elements into them for their satisfaction (6:56-58a). In the Gospel of John, the Lord Jesus said that He is the bread of life (vv. 35, 48), the bread out of heaven (v. 32), the bread of God (v. 33), and the living bread (v. 51) that we may eat Him.

THE FATHER EMBODIED IN THE SON
AND THE SON REALIZED AS THE SPIRIT,
DISPENSING THE PROCESSED TRIUNE GOD
INTO THE BELIEVERS AS LIFE
AND LIFE SUPPLY IN ABUNDANCE

The Father is embodied in the Son, and the Son is realized as the Spirit. In this way, the processed Triune God is dispensed into the believers as life and the life supply in abundance (John 14:9-11, 16-20). The Father in the Son is expressed among the believers, and the Son as the Spirit is realized in the believers. God the Father is hidden, God the Son is manifested among men, and God the Spirit enters into man to be his life, his life supply, and his everything. Hence, the Father in the Son and the Son as the Spirit are man's portion that man may enjoy God.

THE ISSUE OF THE DIVINE DISPENSING
OF THE DIVINE TRINITY AS THE DIVINE LIFE

The Flowing of Rivers of Living Water
as the Bountiful Supply of the Divine Riches

John 7:38-39a says, "He who believes in Me, as the Scripture said, out of his innermost being shall flow rivers of living water. But this He said concerning the Spirit, whom those who believed in Him were about to receive." The issue of our breathing, drinking, and eating Christ is first the flowing of rivers of living water as the bountiful supply of the divine riches.

Fruit-bearing

The second issue of the divine dispensing of the Divine Trinity as the divine life is fruit-bearing (John 15:5, 16a). We are the branches of Christ, who is the vine. As branches we should bear fruit. John 15 does not merely speak of the preaching of the gospel to save sinners, because John is a Gospel of life. In John 15, the preaching of the gospel is the bearing of fruit. Fruit-bearing is the flowing out of the inner life. When the inner life flows out, there is an expression. This expression is fruit-bearing.

Everyone who goes out to lead sinners to be saved must be one with Jesus. If we do not breathe, drink, and eat Jesus, we will not have the authority when we preach the gospel. Our gospel will not be powerful. We must be the breathers, drinkers, and eaters of Jesus. We must have Jesus within us, not merely as a king, but as our breath, water, and food. Many of the dear saints love the Lord and the Lord's recovery very much and are seeking to practice the new way for the church life. However, they are practicing the new way in an old way. When they knock on people's doors for the gospel, they are fearful. Then when they speak with people, they do not command them but rather converse with them in the old way.

Eventually, the people may argue with them, and the time will be wasted. We must not take the old way. To talk to people in this way is not effective.

In Matthew 28:18-19 the Lord said, "All authority has been given to Me in heaven and on earth. Go therefore and disciple all the nations, baptizing them into the name of the Father and of the Son and of the Holy Spirit." We must realize that it is Jesus and not we who initiate our going out. Jesus charged us to go with His authority to disciple the nations. When we go to people, we should say, "Hallelujah! Amen, Lord Jesus. I am going and You are going with me." Then we can tell people, "The Lord Jesus sent me to you to tell you that He is your Savior and you must believe in Him." We can command them to pray, and after they pray, we can command them to be baptized into the name of the Triune God. We have mistakenly believed that we must teach people before they can be saved and baptized. Matthew 28:19 first says that we should disciple the nations, baptizing them into the name of the Father, the Son, and the Spirit. After this, verse 20 says that we should teach them. A mother cannot teach her child before the child is delivered. After the child is delivered, there will be many years to teach him. Whether or not a new believer understands what has happened, his prayer and baptism are accomplished facts, and what he has done in the name of the Lord Jesus counts in God's view.

Lamb-feeding

The issue of the divine dispensing of the Divine Trinity as the divine life is also lamb-feeding (John 21:15, 17). After a new believer is baptized, we should sit down with him to feed him, and come back as soon as possible to have a meeting in his own home. Then we can return regularly to feed him. In feeding the new believers, we should not talk too much. Mothers feed their babies in a very simple way. They know what the babies need, and they know how to feed them in just a few minutes. If we converse with new believers in the old way, they will not be helped.

The first need of the new believers is to breathe the Lord. Therefore, we must feed them with calling on the name of the

Lord. After their baptism we may spend ten minutes to tell them in a simple way, "Now, Jesus is your Lord. He is the Spirit within you. You need to call on Him: Oh Lord Jesus!" This will help them very much. We should teach the new ones in this way. Children practice many things that their mothers teach them, even though they may not understand them.

If possible, on the day after their baptism, we should return to feed the new ones with reading and pray-reading the Bible. We may tell them to read two or three verses from the Gospel of John every day. Then we can open to John 1:1 and read it and pray-read it with them. After this, the new believers will know how to pray-read. We should not help the new ones merely in a human way. We should care for them in a divine way by helping them to keep pray-reading. Then spontaneously we may sing a short song. On another occasion a new one may confess a wrongdoing to us. We can then pray with him, and he may spontaneously have the feeling to rectify the wrongdoing. We do not need to teach the new ones too much. They will learn to do what we do. If we kneel down and pray, they will also kneel down and pray with us. This is the new way, and this is the best way to feed them. The old way is too traditional, habitual, and religious. The new way is practical and very effective. We must not take the old way of conversing, teaching, and charging. We should instead go to the new believers and live a proper Christian life in front of them in a very simple way. They will learn by this and follow us. After a month of meetings in this way, the new ones will grow much.

The Increase of Christ
as the Body of Christ and the Bride of Christ

The issue of breathing, drinking, and eating Jesus is the flow of the living water, fruit-bearing, and the feeding of the lambs. The divine dispensing of the Divine Trinity as the divine life also issues in the increase of Christ, which is the Body of Christ and the bride of Christ (John 3:29-30). John 3:29 says, "He who has the bride is the bridegroom." The bridegroom is Jesus. As the issue of feeding on Him, drinking of Him, and breathing Him in, we will go to bear fruit and feed the new believers, who are the members of His Body, which is His bride. This is the message of the Gospel of John.

We must not merely learn the techniques of bearing fruit and feeding the new ones. We have to live a daily life of breathing, drinking, and feeding on Christ, taking Christ every day as our very element and essence. We must not only receive Him, but also digest Him, assimilate Him, and let Him become the content of our being. Then we will be one with Him. When we go out for the gospel, we will go out in oneness with Him and with His authority. Our going out must also be in the new way, not in the old, traditional, habitual way. We have the living Lord within us. We can always follow Him to know what to do and what not to do. In this way we will baptize sinners and return again and again to feed them. Then we can bring them into our group meetings to be taught and perfected, and they will also spontaneously learn how to prophesy that the church may be built up.

ABOUT THE AUTHOR

Witness Lee was born in 1905 in northern China and raised in a Christian family. At age 19 he was fully captured for Christ and immediately consecrated himself to preach the gospel for the rest of his life. Early in his service, he met Watchman Nee, a renowned preacher, teacher, and writer. Witness Lee labored together with Watchman Nee under his direction. In 1934 Watchman Nee entrusted Witness Lee with the responsibility for his publication operation, called the Shanghai Gospel Bookroom.

Prior to the Communist takeover in 1949, Witness Lee was sent by Watchman Nee and his other co-workers to Taiwan to ensure that the things delivered to them by the Lord would not be lost. Watchman Nee instructed Witness Lee to continue the former's publishing operation abroad as the Taiwan Gospel Bookroom, which has been publicly recognized as the publisher of Watchman Nee's works outside China. Witness Lee's work in Taiwan manifested the Lord's abundant blessing. From a mere 350 believers, newly fled from the mainland, the churches in Taiwan grew to 20,000 in five years.

In 1962 Witness Lee felt led of the Lord to come to the United States, and he began to minister in Los Angeles. During his 35 years of service in the U.S., he ministered in weekly meetings and weekend conferences, delivering several thousand spoken messages. Much of his speaking has since been published as over 400 titles. Many of these have been translated into over fourteen languages. He gave his last public conference in February 1997 at the age of 91.

He leaves behind a prolific presentation of the truth in the Bible. His major work, *Life-study of the Bible,* comprises over 25,000 pages of commentary on every book of the Bible from the perspective of the believers' enjoyment and experience of God's divine life in Christ through the Holy Spirit. Witness Lee was the chief editor of a new translation of the New Testament into Chinese called the Recovery Version and directed the translation of the same into English. The Recovery Version also appears in a number of other languages. He provided an extensive body of footnotes, outlines, and spiritual cross references. A radio broadcast of his messages can be heard on Christian radio stations in the United States. In 1965 Witness Lee founded Living Stream Ministry, a non-profit corporation, located in Anaheim, California, which officially presents his and Watchman Nee's ministry.

Witness Lee's ministry emphasizes the experience of Christ as life and the practical oneness of the believers as the Body of Christ. Stressing the importance of attending to both these matters, he led the churches under his care to grow in Christian life and function. He was unbending in his conviction that God's goal is not narrow sectarianism but the Body of Christ. In time, believers began to meet simply as the church in their localities in response to this conviction. In recent years a number of new churches have been raised up in Russia and in many European countries.

OTHER BOOKS PUBLISHED BY

Living Stream Ministry

Titles by Witness Lee:

Abraham—Called by God	978-0-7363-0359-0
The Experience of Life	978-0-87083-417-2
The Knowledge of Life	978-0-87083-419-6
The Tree of Life	978-0-87083-300-7
The Economy of God	978-0-87083-415-8
The Divine Economy	978-0-87083-268-0
God's New Testament Economy	978-0-87083-199-7
The World Situation and God's Move	978-0-87083-092-1
Christ vs. Religion	978-0-87083-010-5
The All-inclusive Christ	978-0-87083-020-4
Gospel Outlines	978-0-87083-039-6
Character	978-0-87083-322-9
The Secret of Experiencing Christ	978-0-87083-227-7
The Life and Way for the Practice of the Church Life	978-0-87083-785-2
The Basic Revelation in the Holy Scriptures	978-0-87083-105-8
The Crucial Revelation of Life in the Scriptures	978-0-87083-372-4
The Spirit with Our Spirit	978-0-87083-798-2
Christ as the Reality	978-0-87083-047-1
The Central Line of the Divine Revelation	978-0-87083-960-3
The Full Knowledge of the Word of God	978-0-87083-289-5
Watchman Nee—A Seer of the Divine Revelation ...	978-0-87083-625-1

Titles by Watchman Nee:

How to Study the Bible	978-0-7363-0407-8
God's Overcomers	978-0-7363-0433-7
The New Covenant	978-0-7363-0088-9
The Spiritual Man • 3 volumes	978-0-7363-0269-2
Authority and Submission	978-0-7363-0185-5
The Overcoming Life	978-1-57593-817-2
The Glorious Church	978-0-87083-745-6
The Prayer Ministry of the Church	978-0-87083-860-6
The Breaking of the Outer Man and the Release ...	978-1-57593-955-1
The Mystery of Christ	978-1-57593-954-4
The God of Abraham, Isaac, and Jacob	978-0-87083-932-0
The Song of Songs	978-0-87083-872-9
The Gospel of God • 2 volumes	978-1-57593-953-7
The Normal Christian Church Life	978-0-87083-027-3
The Character of the Lord's Worker	978-1-57593-322-1
The Normal Christian Faith	978-0-87083-748-7
Watchman Nee's Testimony	978-0-87083-051-8

Available at

Christian bookstores, or contact Living Stream Ministry

2431 W. La Palma Ave. • Anaheim, CA 92801

1-800-549-5164 • www.livingstream.com